BRITANNICA BEGINNER BIOS

SUSAN B. ANTHONY
PIONEERING LEADER OF THE WOMEN'S RIGHTS MOVEMENT

BARBRA PENNE

Britannica
Educational Publishing

IN ASSOCIATION WITH

ROSEN
EDUCATIONAL SERVICES

Published in 2016 by Britannica Educational Publishing (a trademark of Encyclopædia Britannica, Inc.) in association with The Rosen Publishing Group, Inc.
29 East 21st Street, New York, NY 10010

Distributed exclusively by Rosen Publishing.
To see additional Britannica Educational Publishing titles, go to rosenpublishing.com.

First Edition

Britannica Educational Publishing
J. E. Luebering: Director, Core Reference Group
Mary Rose McCudden: Editor, Britannica Student Encyclopedia

Rosen Publishing
John Kemmerer: Executive Editor
Tracey Baptiste: Editor
Nelson Sá: Art Director
Brian Garvey: Designer
Cindy Reiman: Photography Manager

Library of Congress Cataloging-in-Publication Data

Penne, Barbra.
Susan B. Anthony: pioneering leader of the women's rights movement/Barbra Penne.
    pages cm.—(Britannica beginner bios)
Includes bibliographical references and index.
ISBN 978-1-62275-951-4 (library bound) — ISBN 978-1-62275-952-1 (pbk.) — ISBN 978-1-62275-954-5 (6-pack)
1. Anthony, Susan B. (Susan Brownell), 1820–1906—Juvenile literature. 2. Feminists—United States—Biography—Juvenile literature. 3. Suffragists—United States—Biography—Juvenile literature. I. Title.
HQ1413.A55P46 2016
305.42092—dc23
[B]
                                                                                    2014039761
Manufactured in the United States of America

CONTENTS

Chapter 1
A CHAMPION FOR ALL RIGHTS   4

Chapter 2
GROWING UP QUAKER   8

Chapter 3
EQUAL RIGHTS FOR ALL   12

Chapter 4
LETTING WOMEN VOTE   18

Chapter 5
"FAILURE IS IMPOSSIBLE!"   22

Timeline   28
Glossary   30
For More Information   31
Index   32

CHAPTER ONE

A CHAMPION FOR ALL RIGHTS

Throughout her life, Susan Brownell Anthony worked for the rights of all people. She believed that African Americans should have the same rights as other American citizens. She also believed that women should have the right to vote. She became a leader of the women's rights movement.

Susan B. Anthony spent her life fighting to improve the lives of many people in the United States.

Pioneers of U.S. women's suffrage are Elizabeth Cady Stanton (*left*), Susan B. Anthony (*center*), and Lucretia Mott (*right*).

Women's Suffrage

In many countries today women have the same rights as men. They have the right to own property. They have the right to get an education or to work at any job they choose. They also have the right to vote. The right to vote is called suffrage.

Women have not always had the same rights as men. People called **FEMINISTS** worked for many years to win these rights. Susan B. Anthony was one of the first leaders in the fight for women's suffrage.

Vocabulary

A FEMINIST is any person who believes that men and women should be equal in politics, work, and society.

By the end of Anthony's life, African American men had won the right to vote nationwide. In this 1871 woodcut, African Americans vote in Virginia.

African American Rights

Susan B. Anthony did not only care about the rights of women. She also fought to end slavery in America. People who worked to end slavery were called abolitionists. Anthony was a part of a major abolitionist group. She believed that African Americans should be free. She also thought they should have the right to vote.

During Anthony's life, African Americans and women won many rights in the United States. Other changes came after she died. However, people continue to work for equality today.

> ### Quick Fact
> The word "suffrage" (pronounced SUF-fridge) comes from the Latin word *suffragium*, which means "vote."

CHAPTER TWO

GROWING UP QUAKER

Susan B. Anthony was born on February 15, 1820, in Adams, Massachusetts. Anthony's family was large. She grew up with five brothers and sisters. Her father, Daniel, owned a cotton factory. Her mother, Lucy, stayed at home to raise the children. Anthony's father was part of a religious group called the Quakers.

Quakers and Equality

Quakers are members of a Christian group called the Society of Friends. Quakers believe that each person can feel God on his or her own. They also believe that each person has goodness inside of him or her. Because of this, they believe all people should be equal.

Unlike many other people in the 19th century, Quakers believed strongly in equality for women. This had been an important part of Quaker beliefs since the founding of the religion. Quakers thought women should have the right to go to school and work. In the Anthony family, Anthony's father taught all his children to work and support themselves— even the girls. As a result, Susan B. Anthony got a better education than most American girls in the 1800s.

At Quaker meetings, both women and men preached and shared their beliefs. Equal rights were a common topic.

Quick Fact

Members of the Society of Friends got the name Quakers because they sometimes got so excited when they prayed that they quaked, or shook.

The Society of Friends had special schools where young Quakers could study their religious values. This 1874 group photo is from a Quaker school in Rhode Island.

Quakers Against Slavery

When she was 17, Anthony went to a strict Quaker school near Philadelphia, Pennsylvania. There she studied Quaker **VALUES**. These values taught her that all people were equal.

Quakers also disagreed with slavery. Because they believe each person is equal, they thought slavery was

Vocabulary
VALUES are the beliefs a person has that he or she thinks are important.

unfair. In 1688, Quakers in Pennsylvania held one of the first **PROTESTS** against the slave trade. In 1776, the American colonies became their own country. In 1807, Quakers helped end the slave trade in Great Britain, but slavery still existed in the United States.

When her father's cotton business failed, Anthony became a teacher to help out with money. In 1845, the family moved to a farm in Rochester, New York. Anthony became the head of a school in Rochester in 1846, but she left after only two years. She returned to the family farm in 1849.

Vocabulary

PROTESTS are any public speeches or actions done to show disagreement and to let others know your thoughts or beliefs.

CHAPTER THREE

EQUAL RIGHTS FOR ALL

Anthony's family moved a lot when she was young. She met many new people and learned new things from them. Two of the movements Anthony learned more about were the abolitionist movement and the temperance movement.

Abolitionist Movement

In the mid-1800s, America was divided on the issue of slavery. Many people in the northern states were against slavery. However, many people in the southern states wanted slavery to continue. The people who wanted to end slavery began a movement to abolish, or end, it. This was called the abolitionist movement. Abolitionists wanted a law passed that would free slaves for good.

Quick Fact

Frederick Douglass was a former slave who became a leader of the U.S. abolitionist movement. Douglass told people about his own hard life as a slave. This made many people want to end slavery.

Anthony's family held meetings of abolitionists on their farm. Through them, Anthony met Frederick Douglass and William Lloyd Garrison. Both were leading abolitionists. Garrison was the president of a group called the American Anti-Slavery Society. In 1856, Anthony became the New York **AGENT** for this group.

Vocabulary

An **AGENT** is a person who acts or does business for a group or another person.

Frederick Douglass was an important leader of the abolitionist movement.

Temperance Movement

Another movement Anthony supported was called the temperance movement. "Temperance" means having control over your behavior. The temperance movement taught people to avoid drinking alcohol. Its supporters believed that alcohol caused people to behave badly.

Anthony thought the temperance movement could help protect women. She thought that men who drank too much sometimes mistreated their wives and children.

Many women supported temperance. In this 1879 engraving, a mob of women destroy barrels of alcohol.

Taking Charge

Many men in these movements didn't like Anthony's participation. Often, they would not let her speak in front of crowds because she was a woman. Anthony got tired of not being allowed to speak.

Some criticized Anthony's work for equality. This 1873 cartoon shows Anthony looking like a man in front of a parade of women. On the right, a man holds a baby.

THE DAILY GRAPHIC

AN ILLUSTRATED EVENING NEWSPAPER.

39 & 41 PARK PLACE.

VOL. I—NO. 81.   NEW YORK, THURSDAY, JUNE 5, 1873.   FIVE CENTS.

GRAPHIC STATUES, NO. 17—"THE WOMAN WHO DARED."

In 1851, Anthony met another leader in the cause for abolition, temperance, and women's rights. This was Elizabeth Cady Stanton. In 1852, Anthony and Stanton founded the Woman's New York State Temperance Society. In 1863, they founded the Women's National Loyal League. This group wanted an **AMENDMENT** to the U.S. Constitution to abolish slavery.

Vocabulary
An **AMENDMENT** is a change or addition to a law. So far, there have been 27 amendments to the U.S. Constitution.

Elizabeth Cady Stanton was another important leader in the fight for equality. From 1851 until Stanton's death in 1902, she and Anthony worked closely together.

16

This is a page from the Declaration of Sentiments. The document came from the 1848 convention about women's rights that was held in Seneca Falls, New York.

THE FIRST CONVENTION

EVER CALLED TO DISCUSS THE

Civil and Political Rights of Women,

SENECA FALLS, N. Y., JULY 19, 20, 1848.

———

WOMAN'S RIGHTS CONVENTION.

———

A Convention to discuss the social, civil, and religious condition and rights of woman will be held in the Wesleyan Chapel, at Seneca Falls, N. Y., on Wednesday and Thursday, the 19th and 20th of July current; commencing at 10 o'clock A. M. During the first day the meeting will be exclusively for women, who are earnestly invited to attend. The public generally are invited to be present on the second day, when Lucretia Mott, of Philadelphia, and other ladies and gentlemen, will address the Convention.*

* This call was published in the *Seneca County Courier*, July 14, 1848, without any signatures. The movers of this Convention, who drafted the call, the declaration and resolutions were Elizabeth Cady Stanton, Lucretia Mott, Martha C. Wright, Mary Ann McClintock, and Jane C. Hunt.

They reached their goal in 1865. Congress passed the Thirteenth Amendment, ending slavery. Anthony started working again on winning the right to vote.

Quick Fact

Elizabeth Cady Stanton was an early leader in the fight for women's rights in the United States. In 1848, she and another feminist, Lucretia Mott, held the first women's rights meeting in the United States. Starting in 1851, Stanton worked closely with Susan B. Anthony. Stanton died in New York City on October 26, 1902.

17

CHAPTER FOUR

LETTING WOMEN VOTE

In 1866, Anthony, Stanton, and Lucretia Mott joined a new group called the American Equal Rights Association (AERA). Their goal was to win the right to vote for African Americans and women.

Anthony and others promoted voting rights throughout the country. In this 1870 image, she and another suffragist walk onstage in Ohio to speak.

Quick Fact

In 1867, Anthony and other AERA members traveled to Kansas to try and win the right to vote for both African Americans and women. Despite their efforts, Kansas voted against both state amendments.

The Revolution

In January 1868, Anthony and Stanton began to print a newspaper about women's rights. It was called *The Revolution*. Stanton edited the newspaper's stories. After the Civil War, many suffragists thought they should fight for suffrage for African American men first, then suffrage for all women. Anthony did not agree. *The Revolution* supported women's suffrage.

Later in 1868, the U.S. Congress passed another amendment. The Fourteenth Amendment made African Americans citizens of the United States. Anthony and Stanton were angry that women's rights were being ignored. They asked the AERA to support an amendment for women's suffrage, but that did not happen.

Stanton and Anthony worked together for a long time and grew to become close friends.

Different Priorities

In May 1869, Anthony and Stanton began a new group called the National Woman Suffrage Association (NWSA).

Later that year, other members of the AERA began a group called the American Woman Suffrage Association (AWSA). Both groups had the same goals.

In 1914, members of the **NWSA** show support for a bill that would give women the right to vote. The bill was defeated.

They both wanted suffrage for African Americans and for women. They just believed in different ways of reaching them. The AWSA focused on African American suffrage first. The NWSA wanted to win the right to vote for African Americans and women at the same time. The NWSA also wanted one amendment giving women in the whole country the right to vote. The AWSA worked on getting each state to grant the right separately.

Attempt to Vote

In 1870, the Fifteenth Amendment gave African American men the right to vote. It said that citizens could not be prevented from voting because of their race or color. However, it did not mention women's rights. Most states still did not let women vote.

Anthony and other members of the NWSA were upset. The passage of the Fifteenth Amendment should have meant they could vote, too. Anthony and other NWSA members encouraged women to try to vote in the 1872 election for president. When Anthony voted in the election, she was arrested. She was found guilty and told to pay a fine. She never paid it.

Pictured is the warrant for Susan B. Anthony's arrest for voting in the 1872 presidential election.

"FAILURE IS IMPOSSIBLE!"

This 1892 photograph shows the members of the National Woman Suffrage Association, including Susan B. Anthony.

Anthony began to travel. She went to different states to promote women's suffrage. Western states and territories were more open to her ideas. They saw women's suffrage as a way to get more women to move there and have families. In 1869, the territory of Wyoming gave women the right to vote. Utah followed in 1870, but many other states and territories refused to do the same.

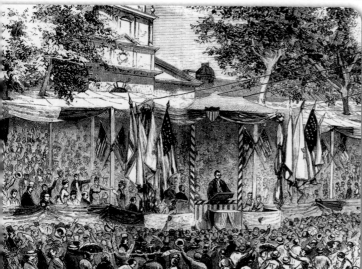

In 1876, the United States celebrated its centennial. Anthony took advantage of the gathering to read a speech demanding women's suffrage.

In July 1876, the United States was celebrating its centennial, or 100-year anniversary. Anthony went to a big celebration in Philadelphia. Vice President Thomas W. Ferry read the Declaration of Independence out loud. Even though she was not supposed to, Anthony read her own speech after Ferry had finished. Her speech demanded equal rights for women. The crowd responded

Quick Fact

In 1876, Anthony and Stanton started to work on a book called *History of Woman Suffrage*. They collected speeches and stories about the women's rights movement. The stories eventually filled six volumes.

On January 6, 1920, Kentucky became the twenty-fourth state to ratify the Nineteenth Amendment.

well to her speech.

Women's Rights Around the World

When Anthony first became an activist, many people did not respect her. Men did not want her to speak at meetings. However, by the 1880s and 1890s, she was more respected. She had become a leader of the women's rights movement around the world.

In 1883, Anthony traveled around Europe, meeting other feminists and sharing her ideas. In 1888, she and several of these women created the International Council of Women (ICW). They met with presidents and other government leaders.

Back home in the United States, Anthony's NWSA and the AWSA joined together again. In 1890 they became the National American Woman Suffrage Association (NAWSA).

The NAWSA worked state-by-state to get women the right to vote. They hoped that if enough states gave women that right, Congress would vote to pass an amendment for the whole country.

Later Years and Death

After traveling around the world promoting women's rights, Anthony finally stopped working. She retired

Since Anthony's death, women in the United States have continued to work for equality. This picture is of a 1970 protest in Washington, D.C., for greater equality for women.

in 1900 at eighty years old. In her last speech, she declared, "Failure is impossible!" Anthony died on March 13, 1906, in Rochester, New York.

Thirteen years later, the U.S. Congress finally voted for an amendment giving women the right to vote. On August 18, 1920, Tennessee became the thirty-sixth state to approve the Nineteenth Amendment. The amendment became a part of the Constitution. Anthony had certainly not failed. Women could finally vote.

Quick Fact

Her work for women's rights made Anthony an American hero. In 1979, she became the first woman featured on U.S. money with the Susan B. Anthony dollar coin.

The Modern Women's Movements

A new women's rights movement began in the 1960s. This movement was commonly called feminism or women's **LIBERATION**. Feminists in the United States formed the National Organization for Women (NOW) in 1966.

Inspired by suffragists such as Anthony, modern feminists work for more rights for women. Women in the United States can vote, but they often face unfairness in politics and work. Important laws passed in the 1960s gave women more equality. Anthony's fight—the fight for greater women's rights—has continued into the 21st century.

Vocabulary
LIBERATION means to be set free.

27

TIMELINE

1820: Susan Brownell Anthony is born in Adams, Massachusetts, on February 20.

1826: The Anthony family moves to Battenville, New York, where Daniel Anthony runs a cotton mill.

1837: Anthony moves to Philadelphia, Pennsylvania, to attend a strict Quaker school.

1839: Anthony moves to New Rochelle, New York, to teach at a Quaker school.

1846: Anthony moves to upstate New York to teach at another school.

1848: Elizabeth Cady Stanton and Lucretia Mott hold the first women's rights meeting in the United States.

1849: Anthony moves to her family's farm near Rochester, New York.

1851: Anthony and Stanton begin working together.

1852: Anthony and Stanton found the Woman's New York State Temperance Society, a group of women who support the temperance movement.

1863: Anthony and Stanton start the Women's National Loyal League, a group that wants to end slavery.

1865: The Thirteenth Amendment to the U.S. Constitution is passed, abolishing slavery.

1866: Anthony, Stanton, and Mott join the American Equal Rights Association (AERA), a group that supports suffrage for both African Americans and women.

1867: Anthony travels to Kansas to support the suffrage movement in that state, but she fails to win passage of a state law to allow women to vote.

1868: Anthony begins printing *The Revolution*, a women's rights newspaper.

1868: The Fourteenth Amendment to the U.S. Constitution is passed, making African Americans citizens of the United States.

1869: Anthony and Stanton leave the AERA and start the National Woman Suffrage Association (NWSA).

1869: The American Woman Suffrage Association (AWSA) is formed.

1870: The Fifteenth Amendment to the U.S. Constitution is passed, giving African American men the right to vote.

1872: The NWSA encourages women to vote in the presidential election. Anthony is arrested for voting.

1873: Anthony is found guilty of voting but refuses to pay the fine.

1876: Anthony reads a speech on women's rights at a U.S. centennial celebration.

1876: Anthony and Stanton begin their book *History of Woman Suffrage*.

1883: Anthony travels around Europe meeting other feminists.

1888: The International Council of Women (ICW) is created.

1890: The NWSA and AWSA join together, forming the National American Woman Suffrage Association (NAWSA).

1900: Anthony retires.

1906: Susan B. Anthony dies on March 13.

1920: The Nineteenth Amendment to the U.S. Constitution is passed, guaranteeing women the right to vote.

GLOSSARY

ABOLITIONIST MOVEMENT An organized series of actions in favor of a law that would end slavery.

ACTIVIST A person who believes in taking strong, powerful actions to show his or her beliefs.

ASSOCIATION An organization or group of people with shared, similar interests or beliefs.

CITIZENS Members of a country or state with special rights protected by laws.

QUAKERS Members of a Christian group that stresses that God is within each person, rejects an ordained ministry or priests, and opposes war.

RETIRED No longer working; ended a professional career.

SLAVERY The practice of owning slaves.

SUFFRAGE The right to vote.

TEMPERANCE MOVEMENT An organized series of acts in favor of self-control, moral behavior, and little or no drinking of alcohol.

FOR MORE INFORMATION

BOOKS

Benoit, Peter. *Women's Right to Vote*. New York, NY: Children's Press, 2014.

Connors, Kathleen. *The Life of Susan B. Anthony* (Famous Lives). New York, NY: Gareth Stevens Publishing, 2014.

Edison, Erin. *Susan B. Anthony* (Great Women in History). North Mankato, MN: Pebble Books, 2013.

Hicks, Peter. *Documenting Women's Suffrage*. New York, NY: Rosen Central, 2010.

Wallner, Alexandra. *Susan B. Anthony*. New York, NY: Holiday House, 2012.

WEBSITES

Because of the changing nature of Internet links, Rosen Publishing has developed an online list of websites related to the subject of this book. This site is updated regularly. Please use this link to access this list:

http://www.rosenlinks.com/BBB/Anth

INDEX

abolitionist movement, 12–13, 16
abolitionists, 7, 12, 13
American Equal Rights Association (AERA), 18
American Woman Suffrage Association (AWSA), 20, 25
Anthony, Daniel (father), 8, 9, 11

Congress, 17, 19, 25, 26
Constitution, 16, 26

education, 5, 9, 10
equality, 7, 8–9, 27

feminists, 5, 17, 25, 27
Fifteenth Amendment, 21
Fourteenth Amendment, 19

History of Woman Suffrage, 23

International Council of Women (ICW), 25

Mott, Lucretia, 17, 18

National American Woman Suffrage Association (NAWSA), 25
National Organization for Women (NOW), 27
National Woman Suffrage Association (NWSA), 20, 21, 25
Nineteenth Amendment, 26

Philadelphia, Pennsylvania, 10, 23
protests, 11

Quakers, 8–11

Revolution, The, 19
Rochester, New York, 11, 25–26

slavery, 7, 10–11, 12, 13, 16, 17
speeches, 11, 23, 25
Stanton, Elizabeth Cady, 16, 17, 18, 19, 20, 23
suffrage, 7, 19, 20, 22, 23

temperance movement, 12, 14, 16
Thirteenth Amendment, 17

United States, 7, 11, 17, 19, 23, 25, 27

values, 10

Woman's New York State Temperance Society, 16
Women's National Loyal League, 16
women's rights, 11, 16, 17, 19, 21, 24–25, 26, 27
women's rights movement, 4, 23, 24, 27